CONFESSIONS OF A PSYCHO POET

HERNIYAH BUTLER

CONFESSIONS OF A PSYCHO POET

PLAYLIST

My Love Mine All Mine – Mitski

Israel's Son – Silverchair

Honeymoon – Lana Del Rey

Girl With One Eye – Florence + The Machine

Dream Brother – Jeff Buckley

Liquid Smooth – Mitski

A Mistake – Fiona Apple

Bleed The Freak – Alice In Chains

I Don't Smoke – Mitski

Nobody Knows – Pastor T.L. Barrett & The Youth for Christ Choir

Is It a Crime – Sade

Please, Please, Please, Let Me Get What I Want – The Smiths

Go to my Spotify playlist for more <3

TRIGGER WARNING

WARNING:

Topic discussions of depression, eating disorders, racism, and more.

CONTENTS

PLAYLIST

For all the weird black girls who lost their minds. Hopefully, we will find them one day.

"Who put this brain inside of me?
It cries
It demands
It says that there is a chance.

It will not say
'no.'"
- Charles Bukowski, The Crunch

NO TITLE NEEDED PT. 1

I hate having to explain myself
But I also hate being misunderstood
It really doesn't matter
Cause nobody listens to me anyway

BUTTERFLY POCKETKNIFE

Beauty and danger cross
At my butterfly pocketknife
I slice and dice
Refuse and resist
My conformity to the masses
Dies in the mist

Beauty and danger
You look at me
And what do you see
"The angry black woman"
That is all I will be
I have my butterfly pocketknife

With me
I will slice and dice at the allegations
And refuse and resist the regulations

What am I?
I'm a butterfly pocketknife
Where beauty and danger cross

I slice and dice
And refuse and resist
My conformity to the masses
Will ALWAYS die in the mist

MY LIFE AS A WOMAN

My life as a woman
Means nothing
If I don't have
Beauty, pain, or ruin
And as I wander through life
Wondering, "What am i doing?"

I continue to question
The things that I have ruined
The things that give me beauty
And the things that give me pain

I end up
Walking and talking
In circles
Repeating myself
And bumping into walls

And still to this day
I am still lost
And so, so confused

A WOMEN'S RAGE IS A GIFT!

The rage that I have
Flowing through my body
Isn't mine
It was passed down by generations of women
In pain and ruin
Torture and murder
Hatred and love
This rage isn't mine
It was just a terrible gift
But I shall use it
I must find a way
To use it
Or it will consume me

SHADES OF RED - ISRAEL'S SON

Shades of red
Rush across your face
Filling the room with your rage
Wading through it
Burns my body
And fries my brain
I pray that it rains
So that it could out the fame

And maybe even the fire in my brain

I hate when this happens
Because it reminds me
Of the times before
And I start to see
The burns on the walls
Scars of the past
And the visions start to come back

It starts to make sense

Why I think of life in terms of
Death, murder, and torture
Because thinking of it any other way
Would be unnatural
For me at least

UGLY SIGHT BY YOUR BED SIDE

Kill me and light me on fire
My burning and rotting flesh
Has the answers to all your desires
You are hungry and full at the same time
You say to yourself "the world is mine"
You tear me apart piece by piece
Until you realize there is nothing left of me
Pieces of the people you have torn apart
Sit by your bed side
The follow you around daily
It's such an ugly sight
Like me rotting away
Begging to see my final light

THE PASSAGE OF MY PEACE OF MIND

You murder my peace of mind
You shoot it, pierce it, and strangle it
And then set it ablaze
Death,
Finally, the torture is over
Right?
Wrong
And just when I think the pain is over
Maggots consume it,
As it decays inside my brain
My peace of mind is nothing but regret and
pieces of rotting flesh
And finally, it's nothing but a skeleton
All that is left are the bones of what it used to be

My peace of mind

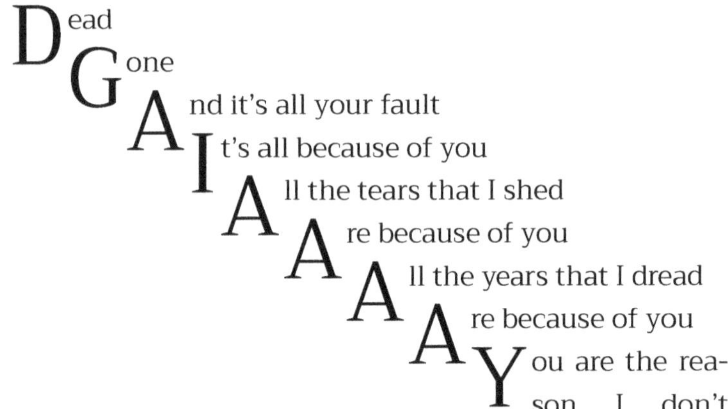

Dead
Gone
And it's all your fault
It's all because of you
All the tears that I shed
Are because of you
All the years that I dread
Are because of you
You are the reason I don't want to get out of bed
It's all you
And then you have the audacity to ask me
"Why do you have an attitude?"
I know why
Do you?

EVERY TIME

Every time I feel criticized
I want to bang my head against the wall
Maybe if I do it
They'll leave me alone

Every time I feel isolated
The lonely air
Which has turned against me
Starts suffocating me

It starts to feel good
Banging my head against the wall
Seeing my skull in real time
It shows me that I'm a real person
That all the emotions I feel are real
It starts to feel good
Suffocating, not only not being
Sable to breathe

But fighting for my life
Which I do every day, but in a separate way

Being myself

Is like the worst form of self-harm
Killing myself to be accepted and appreciated
And the knife I used is just care I have for other people
And they use the same one to cut me deeper

UNDISCOVERED

My body is an undiscovered island
Where nobody has been
And nobody wants to go
Why would you?
It is haunted by the pain of my past.

Do you see it?
The torture on each corner
The pain in every mirror
The demons of the past
Who would want to go there?

Can you hear it?
The banging, kicking
Scratching and screaming
From inside the walls
The rampage running down the halls

Can you see it?
My body in a cage

After the fight I lost
It is scrapped, bruised, and torn
You don't want to see that

You would have to be
One sick person
To want to go there
I would leave
But I've been trapped here for years

This was supposed to be a self-portrait but then I decided to make her a fairy so... it's definitely a self-portrait now

Herniyah Butler

SOMERSET? NO! HELL.

Staying up late
Writing poetry
Up wondering
Why me?

All those years
In that wretched place
Has given me an intense sense
Of self-hate

I see problems
With every piece of myself
My mind, my body, and my soul
There is always something wrong

The on-going war in my brain
That has no end
If I'm able to remember
How I was treated back then

The pain that I felt
Put a gun to my head

And give me the choice
I definitely would not do it again

I would rather die a slow, painful death
Rather than go back there again
It's practically the same thing
Cause I have not been alive since then

NO TITLE NEEDED PT. 2

I haven't been sad in a while
Not because everything is okay
But because
Nothing feels real anymore

MY SOUL NOT MY BODY

Every time I feel hungry
I'm going to write
I need something
To feed my soul
Instead of my body

Doesn't matter
What I write
It doesn't matter
What I do
As long as I don't eat food

The pain in my heart
When I look in the mirror
Is not worth feeling full
As long as I look like this
I am empty and starving

TAKE THE BOX

Take the box
With my heart inside
I don't use them anyway
I haven't felt anything in a while
Might as well take my soul too
Take the whole thing
I will sit waiting here for you
to bring it back

You'll find a better use for them
I haven't been using them well
But I would rather you take
My pain and tears
I guess you need what I don't use

It's okay I've gotten along fine without it
Not exactly fine
But I've gotten along
I have floated by

Take the box
Take my heart

Take my peace of mind
And take my soul to

All you want is what you can have
Use it better than I have
I know i say “It’s okay”
But you know you hear me screaming
As you take it away

LONELY CORPSE

Alone
You keep telling me I'm going to be alone
Forever
Who would want to deal with me?
Die alone
That's what I'm going to do
But it's okay
Cause I'm already alone

I have been fighting this fight on my own
Few noticed
They just tell me what I have done wrong
And I haven't felt alive in a while
I've said this before
I'm kind of just floating by
Just going through the motions

So really
I have already died alone
But thank you so much
For bringing that to my attention
But there is no use in talking to a lonely corpse

I just wanted to make something kind of trippy so this was the outcome

Herniyah Butler

ME BEING MESSY PT. 1

All those years in that hellhole
Told me I was going to die alone
I don't need to hear it from you

FREAK OF NATURE

The ribbons in my hair
Have unraveled
And fallen to the ground
Decomposing
Buried underground
My tears water them
Blooming the flower
Of my adolescence
Nature killers
Took it
home

And sat it in the sun too long
It welts away
And with it so does my soul
Somehow, I still go on
Me, a walking dead plant
Just standing still
A walking dead plant
A freak of nature

"THE STRONG BLACK MAN"

My father,
"The Strong Black Man"
The perfect stereotype
Angry with the world
Anything but white

What happens when we look
Beneath the surface
And see the pain, trials, and tribulations
That's he has gone through
Just to be... "The Strong Black Man"

And when he's calm
He's actually really cool
But "The Man" don't like him like that
So, they light the fuse
Cause you know he must be "The Strong Black Man"

What exactly is a "Strong Black Man"

Is it even though your pain
Is flowing through your veins
And burning right through your skin
You remain straight- faced
And let the darkness consume you from within

We as observers
Sit and we analyze this figure
Of "Strong Black Masculinity"
And we see the true weakness
Lying beneath

See "The Man"
Wants us to believe
That "The Strong Black Man"
Is real because that is how they see
The black man
Strong, angry, violent, and willing

But black men are people too
Not these soldiers you want them to be

They have trained my father
To be this soldier
And broken him in war
He is suffering, broken, and torn
And he does what society does to him

To the people who love him the most

ROCK ON, BLACKBIRD

I rock on
Even with the tears I cry
I wipe them away
And put my eyeliner on
Just to show the world
How strong I am
Broken inside
But strong, I hide
With the lies
I tell just to get by

SWAMPY SEA

Return me
To the swampy sea
Then come back
And rescue me

Let me drown
Let me struggle to breathe
Leave me with the moss
The birds and the bees

Then bring me back
You're coming back, right?

ME BEING MESSY PT.2

"You've changed so much"
Sorry I grew a personality
You should try it sometime
But yeah
You enjoy being a stereotype
And I will continue to be "white"

I have much bigger plans
Than what you want for me anyway
You can stay in your small-minded world
I am on to so much bigger

HONEYMOON

Dreaming away your life
Since I was little girl
Blocking out the pain
With the fantasies of a new world

The people around me
Told me,
"The life you have is just fine"
But from an early age
I knew something wasn't right

Why do I cry at night
Why do I have this pain inside
Something just doesn't feel right

This life isn't mine
This life wasn't meant for me
It was meant for someone without dreams

DREAMERS – TWO SIDES OF THE SAME COIN

Dreamers don't get to live
Dreamers die
But it's okay because
We live through our dreams
Or
Dreamers never die
We live on through dreams
As it seems, we are two sides of the same coin

"DREAMING AWAY YOUR LIFE" - LANA DEL REY

Dreaming away my life
Has gotten me in trouble
I forgot to live my real life
I feel as though the days
Are passing me by
I am going to be 18 next year
And I have spent the last 13 years
Dreaming of what my life could be

But now I am stuck because
I don't know how to get out of this place

KNOCK ON WOOD

Every hallway I walk through
Is empty
Every pool I swim in
Is shallow
All the wood I knock on
Is hollow

Why not me?
When is it my turn?
To walk a busy hall
Comforted by friends

Why not me?
When is it my turn
To swim
In a deep, blue, and clear ocean
Surrounded by the sea creatures
I can call my companions

"Knock on wood, you'll jinx yourself"
They say
I am jinxed forever

I knock on wood
To save my self
But all of it is hollow
Not true nor sincere
Why not me?

When is it my turn please
Just one time
Can I knock on wood
And feel fulfilled, feel real, feel comforted
Please that's all I ask

I AM A NATURAL MERMAID

Born underwater
Floated to the shore
Now I wander through life wanting more

Left my tail underwater
I'm worth more without it

I DON'T SMOKE

The things you say to me
You forget and move on
And they stay with me
Forever
They twist and turn in my head
Burning a hole through my brain
Bring back up the pain of what you said
Just last week
Making me feel like throwing up
And throwing it right back at you
But I don't,
I sit and become a punching bag for you

What have I done to you
Actually, you don't need to explain
I have lost my desideratum to know why
You treat me this way
It's just my fault

You don't need to say you're sorry

I know you are not
But even though you're not
I forgive the bad
When you're good
And I forgive the bad
When you're worse
Cause I love you,
Even if I am just a
pain to you

DEAL WITH IT

I dislike myself
More than you dislike me
I disgust myself
More than I disgust you
I loathe myself
More than you loathe me
You don't like who I am
Neither do I
Nothing either
of us can do

To change that
So just deal with it
We both just have to deal with it
Deal with me
Me more than you
It is just temporary for you
For me it's permanent
A lifelong sentence

TENDENCY TO DISGUST

Please forgive me for my tendency to disgust
It's a must
For the frigid winter lonely air
Keeping everyone away from me
Until it becomes dusk

A FORMAL APOLOGY

You could have sworn you were a child
And I was the adult
I, a little girl, was supposed to fight your battles
For you
And if I did not, I was the villain
So, I did
I was going to war for you
And the same weapons I formed upon
Someone else for you
You used on me
But it was okay because
You were just a kid
You didn't know any better

But I cannot defend you anymore
I surrender, I am putting my guns down
I cannot fight for you anymore
So, I would like to apologize to everyone
Who had to feel the wrath
Of your army of one

This is an art piece that I did back in 2020 or 2021. I got fourth place in an art competition for this

Herniyah Butler

WEST COAST DREAMS

It's Cali, baby!
The land of Jim Morrison
Where we take a walk
On Love Street
The Land of Lana Del Rey
As we ride with the birds
On the summer breeze
The land where a girl so far away

Dreams of being
The dream I have of
Sitting on the floor
Of the Chateau Marmont
Listening to records
With you, my whole heart
The records I play
Tell the story of the pain

I used to feel
I hear it, loud and clear
But you know what?
It doesn't affect me anymore

Because I'm here

Hello, hi, this is awkward, I really don't know what to say but we will give it a shot. My name is Herniyah Elizabeth Butler, I'm from Miami, Florida, and I am seventeen years old (but by the time you read this I will be eighteen). My favorite colors are dark purple, cherry red, and black (in that order). I played a lot of sports in childhood and teen years including cheer, competitive cheer, dance, track, cross country, soccer, and a little bit of volleyball. Most of those sports, except cheer and dance, were my mother's ideas. Speaking of mother, let's talk about parents, my mother is Afro-Cuban, and my father is just a mixture of things, but he just identifies as Black. My parents sent me to a predominantly white Hispanic charter school, after believing too many stereotypes about public school. Going to that school truly ruined me, shaped me into who I am today because I had to rebuild myself completely (still working on it). Once I graduated from there, my mom put me and my sister in online school, and after a year or so, she decided to home school us herself.

In my time at home, not going to many places, I started discovering diverse types of music. The kickstart of that was either Willow Smith, The Runaways Movie, or Lana Del Rey, but the truthful answer is Willow Smith. Willow Smith just made so many distinct types of music and truly opened a new world for me because I was told music like that was weird or taboo. My family thought I was so strange for listening to Rock and Indie music, but I truly felt understood when I listened to it. Like Lana Del Rey, Rage Against the Machine (specifically Zack De La Rocha), and Willow Smith are some of the many reasons I started appreciating lyricism and writing poetry. Also, because "my saddest was too big" and I had to get it out somehow or I don't know what I would do. Maybe cause mass destruction? I don't know. My biggest dream is to make an album, an album that can help or change someone's life like Grace by Jeff Buckley, Ultraviolence by Lana Del Rey, House of Balloons by the Weeknd, When the Pawn by Fiona Apple, or Willow by Willow Smith and so many more did for me. I just hope that dream comes true because that would be utterly amazing. Anyway, I just decided to collect my poems and put them in a book for you all and I hope you like it.

Fun Fact: My brother told me that when I finish writing this book, he would buy me Calico Critters, Sonny Angels, and Smiskis. Love you, Jaccare! Also, shout out for dropping the funds. Also, shout out to my mother because she thought that putting this together would take another year.... HA! It did not! Love you, Mommy!

Herniyah Butler

www.ingramcontent.com/pod-product-compliance
Lightning Source LLC
Chambersburg PA
CBHW041648150726
48005CB00015BB/2517

* 9 7 9 8 2 1 8 4 9 3 7 6 9 *